The Discipline Coach

If you're thinking discipline is
keeping them in check, sorting
them out, showing them what's
good for them, because it's for their
own good, because it's what the
youth of today are so sorely lacking

... you've got the wrong book

The
Discipline Coach

 **Jim Roberson**
edited by Ian Gilbert

Published by
Independent Thinking Press, Crown Buildings, Bancyfelin, Carmarthen,
Wales, SA33 5ND, UK
www.independentthinkingpress.com

Independent Thinking Press is an imprint of Crown House Publishing Ltd.

First published 2012. Reprinted 2013.

British Library of Cataloguing-in-Publication Data
A catalogue entry for this book is available from the British Library.

Print ISBN 978-1-78135-005-8
Mobi ISBN 978-1-78135-036-2
ePub ISBN 978-1-78135-037-9

Edited by Ian Gilbert
Printed and bound in the UK by
Stephens & George, Dowlais, Merthyr Tydfil

To my parents James and
Nettie Roberson, I know the world has not
always been an ideal place, but thank you
for being my ideal parents.

Acknowledgments

I would like to thank Caroline Lenton and Tom Fitton at Independent Thinking Press, also a big hug to my friend, editor and boss, Ian Gilbert. You folks are professionals, loved the process, let's do it again soon!

To my lovely wife, Teresa, folks I'm blessed I have it all, thanks for all the typing and pre-editing. To my children, thanks for the support, Maria and Gemma my typing crew, David and Courtney, sales department. Wow, thanks!

Contents

Foreword

How often do you start sentences – or hear others start sentences – with the words 'Not my …'? Sentences like, not my fault, not my problem, not my responsibility, not my job …?

And how often do you look around and wish things were different?

I realised way back in my first ever 'proper' job that there were two sorts of people in the world of work. There were DDMs and DMDs. DDMS were the Don't Do: Moans. They didn't like what was going on but they never did anything about it. Apart from moaning. In my third ever 'proper' job I soon discovered that this is what staffrooms were for.

DMDs didn't like it either but, rather than sitting around berating the world and all who lived in it for not being good enough, they found ways of getting on and making it better. Making it different. Making a difference. These were life's Don't Moan: Dos. These are very special people and should be cherished.

Making a difference, however, is hard work. It means nipping all those 'Not my …' sentences in the bud. It's not about what isn't my fault, problem, responsibility or job, but all about doing everything I need to in order to bring the world kicking and screaming in line with all that it can be. It means not sitting around making myself feel good because I am surrounded by others who have the same complaints, mitherings, whinges and excuses I have. It means applying myself to making myself better each day in order to make things better each day.

And that takes discipline.

Jim Roberson has discipline. He is an enigma. He is a force of nature. He is, in the words of so many of the young people whose lives he has helped transform, a 'f@*#%ing legend'! And he is very much the sort of person who, as his fellow Americans like to say, 'walks the talk'.

I have known Jim for many years now, ever since we first met when I was doing an INSET session at the school where he was based, a school in one of the rougher parts of Portsmouth on England's south coast. At this school, Jim was 'The Discipline Coach'. Not in a 'Do your work or we'll send for Mr Roberson and he'll sort you out!' sort of way. Quite the opposite. Discipline isn't something, in Jim's world, we do to others. Disciplining someone just teaches them that they didn't work hard enough at not getting caught. That it's OK to be naughty until someone stops you and if no one stops you then just carry on. That the reason you haven't got that nice pair of trainers is because life is crap. And the reason for that is everyone else.

Jim's approach, rather, is not about what we do to others but what we do for ourselves. Over the years, I have seen Jim transform the lives of many, many young people, whether it's helping them focus on doing better in their studies, staying on the straight and narrow at school, playing that sport that much better, getting out of crime, contributing more as a member of the family, as a member of a community, getting a job, aiming higher, going further. He has helped turn around the lives of so many people and at the core of this is his philosophy of discipline. It is this philosophy that we have tried to distil into this book. And do it in a way that captures Jim's spirit, his voice and his relentless energy. To do this we have had to create a very special sort of book. Different from all the other 'books for teachers' that fill the shelves, often unread. It's not a 'How to' book or a 'Top Ten Tips' guide for busy teachers. It's actually a philosophy book with an autobiography wrapped up inside it for good measure.

What we want is for you to read it and enjoy it. And that in doing so, it will give you the reassurance to be even better at what you do. That it will offer you new insights to bring to bear on the young people whose lives you can touch. That it will help you see how much more we can all do for those young people. And that the biggest thing we can do for them is to remind them how much they can do for themselves. If they have the discipline to do so.

Ian Gilbert
Craig-Cefn-Parc
July 2012

Discipline represents original native endowment turned, through gradual exercise, into effective power. The aim of education is precisely to develop intelligence of this independent and effective type – a disciplined mind. Discipline is positive and constructive.

John Dewey, *How We Think* (1910)

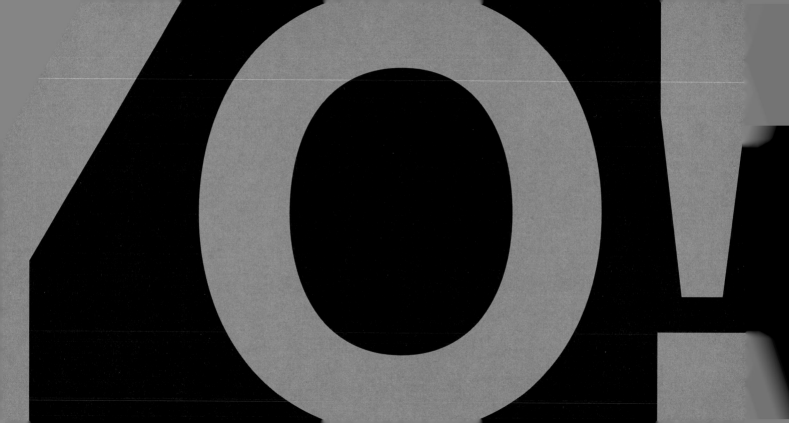

Let's get some things straight.

A few ground rules.

DISCIPLINE

The sort of discipline I'm talking about may not be the sort of discipline you're thinking about.

If you're thinking discipline is to keep them in check, to sort them out, to show them what's good for them, because it's for their own good, because it's what the youth of today are so sorely lacking …

… then you're reading the wrong book.

'Discipline is positive and constructive.'

John Dewey

There was once a quite amazing American college football coach called

Lou Holtz.*

He is what is known where I'm from as a Hall of Fame coach. **One of the best.**

* Me and American football go back a long way.
I first came across the amazing Coach Holtz
when I was coach of a high school football team
in Tuckahoe, New York.

1983

He had
a definition
of discipline
that is right
at the heart
of all the
work I do,

that best
sums up for
me what this
magical
thing called
discipline
is all about.

He said:

'Discipline is not what you do **to** yourself, but what you do **for** yourself!'

Lou Holtz

Not what you do to yourself or what someone else does to you.

You're not there to discipline young people.

What does this teach our students?

Do what you want till you get found out?

Anything is OK till someone tells you it isn't?

My behavior is someone else's responsibility?

I don't think so!

Discipline is not what you do to yourself or what anyone else does to you.

It's what you do for yourself.

You see - I tell the young people I work with - you are your own secret weapon.

You are the answer.

You are the one you've been waiting for.

You just need
to be prepared
to do what you need
to in order
to set your
potential
free.

In the words of basketball coach Bobby Knight

**'You need to
do what needs to
be done,
when it needs
to be done
how it needs,
to be done.'**

**And then
do it
that way**

all the time.

But that takes discipline.

Self-discipline

The discipline
to be your own coach,
your own boss.

Your best friend,
your fiercest critic,
your greatest ally.

To hold yourself to the highest
standards

To take the opportunities
when they arise

And to follow through.

BRONXVILLE PUBLIC SCHOOL
BRONXVILLE, NEW YORK 10708

JOHN E. HELFRICH
SUPERINTENDENT OF SCHOOLS

June 13, 1977

Dear Jim,

It seems as if I am always writing to congratulate
you on some outstanding performance. It was super that
you were selected for both the county and league teams.
I might add that it was well deserved, too.

Jim, it has been a privilege having you in the
Bronxville School. You have added a great deal to our
student body this year. Thank you for participating so
fully in our school.

I certainly wish you well in the future. It is my
hope that you will find a spot where you can contribute
as you did here. I am not worried about your future as
I know you will be a success at whatever you undertake
if you really want to.

Have a good summer.

Sincerely,

Jack Helfrich

P.S. Congrats on the "News" team too. Great!

Mr. James Roberson
Bronxville High School
Bronxville, New York

So proud of this letter from school.

1977

To expect only the best for yourself
and from yourself

To be the one you can
always rely on

**To do what
needs to be done,
when it needs to be done,
and how it needs to be done.**

And to do it that way all the time.

So discipline isn't about a teacher having a go at a young person.

It's not about being punished.
Held up as an example.
Made to feel bad.
ANGRY.

Small.

And while we're on the subject, let me tell you something else that discipline isn't.

Discipline

(and this one makes my blood boil)

is not about the B*-Word

*Behavior (or behaviour – makes no odds. It's still the B-word)

When I'm working with groups of young people –

Difficult,

Disaffected,

Disconnected

Young people –

This is what I say to them:

'Your behavior is not important today. As a matter of fact I don't care how you behave. But if you show me the same respect I show you, if you conduct yourself with respect and self-respect, we will have a great time!'

That's what I say.

And do you know what?
I never have a problem with behavior.

And it all boils down to three words:

**Respect
Accountability
Preparation**

RAP

I was flying back to the UK recently and I read about a primary school in Cornwall that was doing amazing things. It was a school I had visited to work with the young folks.

The reporter asked them what the secret of their success was. They said:

'We RAP!'

The plane may have landed soon after that but as far as I was concerned I was flying higher than ever.

RAP is something I had shared with those young folks and is one of the first things I cover when I'm working with any group of people, whether it's learners in school, young offenders, or football players. Anyone.

And it works

RAP goes right to the heart of what discipline is all about.

Successful discipline.

Getting discipline right.
And you don't find it in no darn B-word:

**Respect
Accountability
Preparation**

That's what RAP is all about.

**Respect
me.**

**Respect
yourselves.**

We'll get along fine.

Respect lasts you a lifetime.
It's morals.
It's manners.

It's about coaching students to feel good enough
about themselves – because a better *you* starts
with a respectful *you*. It means showing everyone
respect, including yourself.

Respect is at the heart of cutting down on
exclusions in schools.*

*Why do we exclude young people from schools?
Or even classrooms?
Do we think that by missing lessons they will catch up?
I have never kicked a kid out of one of my lessons.
Never. Nor should you. Be creative.

Teach respect,
don't simply expect it.

Model it.
Live it.

You want respect from them?

Give respect to them.

I have never met a kid that didn't
show me respect.*

*But then again, I have never met a kid who I didn't show respect to.

Every time they're messing around,
acting dis-respectfully,
as they will from time to time*

And you wade in
Shouting
Threatening
Stressing

*They're kids. It's what they do.

Think about what you are doing to their brains.

For learning to be effective you want their neocortex to kick in – the clever, thinking brain.

But when you shout and threaten you activate their reptilian brain.

Fight.

Flight.

And their emotional brain starts to overheat.

And they start to see red.

Your threats stir up chemicals that hijack their brains.

Don't make 'em mad.

Make 'em think.

IT THROUGH

Here are three tools I use
to help young people
think before they act,
before they do something
they'll regret.

1.   Consider All Factors
CAF

This is relevant whether you're talking about
disrupting lessons,
poor attendance,
bullying,
crime,
having unprotected sex,
or leaving school with no qualifications.

**Ask: What are the implications of this
action? Come on, think it through.**

2.   Consequence + Repercussion
C + R

Nothing happens in isolation. Everything leads to something.
Consequences are what happen to you in the short term.

If you don't do the work that is expected of you, you get a detention as a consequence.*

Repercussions are something that kick in long term.

*For which you do
or don't show up.

Long term by not doing the work,
you'll fail that exam.

You fail your exams,
you limit your life choices.

You limit your life chances,
you limit your life.

That's long term.

You don't do the work = you don't learn
to read or write = your life is limited
before it's even fully started.

That's one helluva repercussion for going out for the evening instead of having the discipline to do your work.

No GCSEs.

Low reading skills.

Poor math skills.

Smoking.

Crime.

Teen parenting.

They all have long-term repercussions even if you don't see the short-term consequences.

3.   Take Care of Business
TCB

Do you respect yourself enough to do what needs to be done, when it needs to be done, how it needs to be done, and do it that way all the time?

This is Taking Care of Business.

Put
up.Shut up. **Do
it.**

And while we're thinking in acronyms here's another one:

$$T + C = U$$

Teaching+Coaching = Understanding

T:
Teaching

Introduce them to the ideas in this book. They're good ones. They work. I know that because I've used them with thousands of young people over the years. But don't think that is enough. Teaching them about discipline is only one step. But I ain't no Discipline Teacher.

I'm the Discipline Coach.

C:
Coaching

Support them as they use what you have taught them and apply it on an ongoing basis in their own lives.

Help them when they get stuck. Pick them up when they fall. Encourage them when they falter. Have higher expectations of them than anyone in their life has ever had. Expect nothing but the best from them. Expect them to expect nothing but the best from themselves.
You know, coaching.

U:
Understanding

You teach them. You coach them. They get it.

Got to have them both for kids to get it, man.
Teaching and coaching.
Got to have
both.

SELF

DISCIPLINE

Anyway, back to RAP.
So, you model respect and encourage them to
show it to you, to their peers,
to themselves.
But it's not your job to ensure they show respect.
It's theirs.

The A in RAP is *accountability*.

To be held to account for what you do.
What you choose to do.
What you opt to do.

If you can't do the time, don't do
the crime.

But to help them become accountable we have to give them the opportunity to become responsible.

How will they ever learn accountability if we don't trust them with anything in life?

'No, you can't take those exercise books home. We don't trust you.'

'No, you can't work in the library. You'll stay here where I can see you.'

'Yes, of course you can work on the computer.'*

*But we've blocked most of the websites just in case ...

Why do we persist in taking away from young people opportunities to help them learn accountability?

How do you teach accountability and raise aspirations in young people who have never owned a passport?

Who have never left their hometown?

Who society has run down and written off?

You take them to New York*

*The trip was open to all but if you had poor attendance you had to improve it to go. If you had a classroom discipline issue you had time to improve and the trip staff would also work with students to help them get it right. No excuses. Working to change. And parents were told that they should expect their children to do a few more chores in return for the spending money. Lesson? You earn opportunities. Nobody gives you a free trip to New York.

I ran two trips a year to New York for several years. We would land at about 4pm, get to the hotel around 7pm, settle till 9pm and then go out to Times Square and go trainer shopping. Wow! Back to hotel around midnight and no one could sleep with the excitement of tomorrow. We would visit the United Nations and Ground Zero. We spoke with parents about expectations on the trip – language, dress, conduct on the bus, at the airport, on the airplane, in the hotel. Folks, every year I would receive great comments about our students. I even received a letter from Virgin Atlantic complimenting the conduct of our students.

Difficult, disaffected, poor kids from the wrong side of the tracks.

School trips help to create aspirations. Trusting students to be responsible gives them the opportunity to develop accountability.

And the P in RAP: ***preparation***.

This is a biggie. This separates those with aspirations from those who achieve.

This separates those with motivation from those who actually do something.

This is the difference between success and failure.

It can turn a losing team into a winning team, an underdog into a champ.

In the words of Malcolm X:

'The future belongs to those who prepare for it today.'

I'd rather have **preparation** over motivation. Everybody likes to play; few like to practice.

Preparation is key. I have found that the more I prepare the closer I get to getting it right.

Or, in the words of one my heroes, record-breaking American football coach Paul 'Bear' Bryant:

'It's not the will to win, but the will to prepare to win that makes the difference.'

CROSSOVER

It's not about exercise.
It's about discipline.

How can children use RAP once they have learned to RAP with you?

In their behavior in and around school.
In the classroom to combat 'behavior' issues.
In their relationships with their teachers.
In their relationships with their parents.
In their relationships with each other.
In their relationships with themselves.*

*Learning RAP does wonders for kids with low self-esteem.

And, one of my favorites, they can use it in sport.

Which brings me to what I call *crossover*. This is about taking principles and ideas from sport and applying them directly to school. It works with all young people, but it works especially well with those who are great at sport but lousy at school.

Every other Saturday I work for a Youth Offending Team. We run sessions for young people, 11 to 17 year olds, who are in trouble with the law. They are with me for an hour and they have it tough: running, sprints, sit-ups, push-ups …

For most of them it's the only physical exercise they do. Ever. But the session's not about exercise. It's about discipline. The past is done; the future is here. We get them to make choices. Decisions that don't just affect them, but concern the whole group.

Then, folks, we help them to stick to the deal and be accountable for working hard and doing what is asked. For example, they may have to decide between ten laps jogging or five laps sprinting. They determine what they do. We help reinforce the deal with positive support. Moral support. We practice the art of making them feel good about themselves and the choices they make. 'Discipline is not what you do to yourself but what you do for yourself.'

Do you have the discipline to do your laps?

To do your push-ups?

Do you have the discipline to
stick with your decision?

See, folks, these tools can be applied daily.
Start them, develop them, and you will start
to see change. Positive change starts with
understanding that discipline is not what you do
to yourself but what you do for yourself.

In the classroom the same ethos applies.

Do you respect yourself enough,
do you have what it takes,
do you have the discipline to
come to school every day,
get to your lessons on time,
get there ready to learn, and
get to stay there?

That's crossover.

The thing is, we all get 24 hours.

It's the only fair thing. It's equal to all, whether you're an A* student or a school dropout.

Whether you're 50 Cent or Joe Average.

We're all equal
in the face of the clock.

The rarest gift you will ever receive
is also the most common.

It's a brand
new day.

The question is:

Are you disciplined enough to make
the most of your 24 hours each day?

Every day?

Think about your most
disaffected students.*

Where are they showing
discipline in their lives already?

Sport, music, skateboarding,
computer games, crime?

What opportunity for crossover
is there?

*There's another word we throw around that makes me mad. 'Disaffected'. As if that is something the child does. No, we 'dis-affect' young people. What are you doing to 're-affect' them?

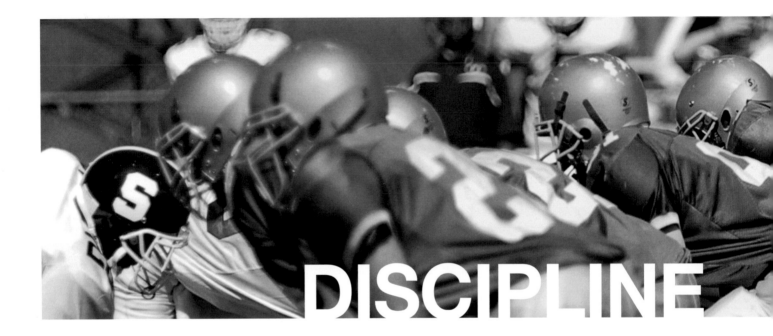

ACTION PLAN

During my career coaching
American football …

… I have had two great jobs:

Head Coach of Tuckahoe High School, New York (1983–1984) and Head Coach, of the Southern Sundevils in Portsmouth, UK (1998–2006).

When I arrived, both programs were going through rough patches. During my first season at Tuckenhoe High we won one, lost seven. In the second season we won seven, lost one, drew one. And we were Bowl Champs in Westchester County, New York. Hell, yeah, that's as good as it sounds.

In my first season with the Southern Sundevils we won six, lost five, and reached the playoffs. In the second season, my first as Head Coach, we were league champions. We did that three times in total.

Each time, the first step was never about the football, but it was also *all* about the football. Step one was to establish an ethos of discipline.

As a coach, the first step to developing champions is to get them to buy into being champions. This leads to doing the things,

all the things,

that make you a champion.

And this is where the windmill comes in handy.

This sign:

represents a windmill.

It's about strength.
Resilience.
The ability to keep going no matter what life throws at you.
Turning. Turning.
It is a symbol from my African-American heritage – about the power we once
had and the ability to face life's difficulties.

After all, discipline is about
keeping on keeping on.

No matter what life is
throwing at you.

When I'm working with young people I use the windmill symbol as the central structure for what I call their Discipline Action Plan. It will help them achieve anything they want to.

Anything. As Will Smith likes to say:

'Nothing is unrealistic.'*

*How often do teachers decide for young people what is or isn't within their grasp? Stop it. Don't limit them with your limited view of the possible. Listen to Will Smith.

Discipline Action Plan

The first stage.

There is *motive*.

MOTIVE

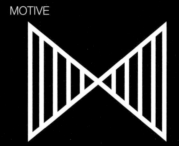

Tell me what you want, what you really, really want?

A nice house?
A great salary?
A flash car?*
Five A–Cs at GCSE?

Without the compelling motive – or as Ian Gilbert calls it, the WIIFM or What's In It For Me? – then all this is just a waste of time.

To get what you want you've got to *know* what you want.

*Although as my dad says,

**'The man's got to
get out of the car'.**

Here is a good way of helping them identify that all-important WIIFM:

Write down the ideal job you would like in the future.
What type of job is it?
What kind of life will it give you?
What 'stuff' would you want (car, house, holidays, etc.)?

Then the biggie:
How much money would you like to make?

Then the *real* biggie:
How will you be contributing?

(I tell them at this point to watch out for Spirit Snipers. The people who say you can't. You won't. It'll never happen. The people who laugh at you. Young people call them 'friends'. Beware of what the Spirit Snipers want. They want your spirit.)

Next you ask this question: 'How could you be using school to help you achieve that future?'

You can usually hear a pin drop at this point.

Then I tell them:

If you love what you do you'll never work a day in your life.

Kareem Abdul-Jabbar, former US basketball pro and
the NBA's all-time highest scorer,* said this:

'Working for a living is easy.
Not working for a day in
your life takes effort.'

So, to achieve that future that you really want,
what are you going to do about it?
In fact, not just do – change.

* 38,387 points – WOW!

Write down five changes you will start making today.

Will it be

Your attitude?
Your behavior?
Your effort?
Your approach?
Your actions?
Your choices?

Three of them are changes you are going to make at school and two of them are changes you are going to make at home.

I want them to

admit

they need to change

then

commit

to the change they need to make

The past is gone.

The future is getting better.

The present is where the change happens to make this possible.

That's one helluva motive!

Next there's our old friend …

The D-word: *discipline.*

Not 'What do you have to do to achieve your goal?'

but 'What do you have to discipline yourself to do
in order to achieve whatever your motive is?'

After that we get under the surface.
Succeeding isn't just about what you think. Nor is
it only about what you do.

Success is about what you feel.

MOTIVE DISCIPLINE

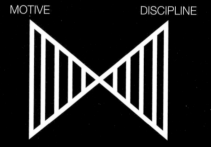

So next is *affect.*

How will you feel about yourself when
(not 'if') you achieve your goal?

How will you feel on results day when you get the grade you worked for? How
will your parents feel about you. And themselves? What about your teachers,
how will they feel about you? And, most importantly, how will you feel about
you?

MOTIVE   DISCIPLINE

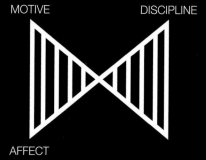

AFFECT

Finally, there's another old friend: *preparation*.

Preparation doesn't mean simply being 'up for it'. It's about having a plan.

After all, you know what they say:

'Failing to plan is planning to fail.'

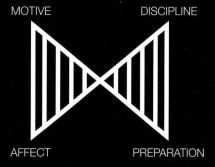

MOTIVE   DISCIPLINE

AFFECT   PREPARATION

When I'm working with young people I show them a picture of the University of Michigan football stadium. It is known as 'The Big House' and it seats 109,901 people.

Then I ask the big question:

If you were playing a game in front of over 100,000 people do you think you would plan what you intend to do?

Too right you would!

Preparation is key.
I want students to rely on preparation not motivation.

Now take your Discipline Action
Plan and stick it where you can
see it
every day.

That way
you can focus on what you want,
what you are prepared to do to
achieve it,
what you will feel like having
achieved it
and what you need to do in order
to
achieve it.

Then go out
and achieve it.

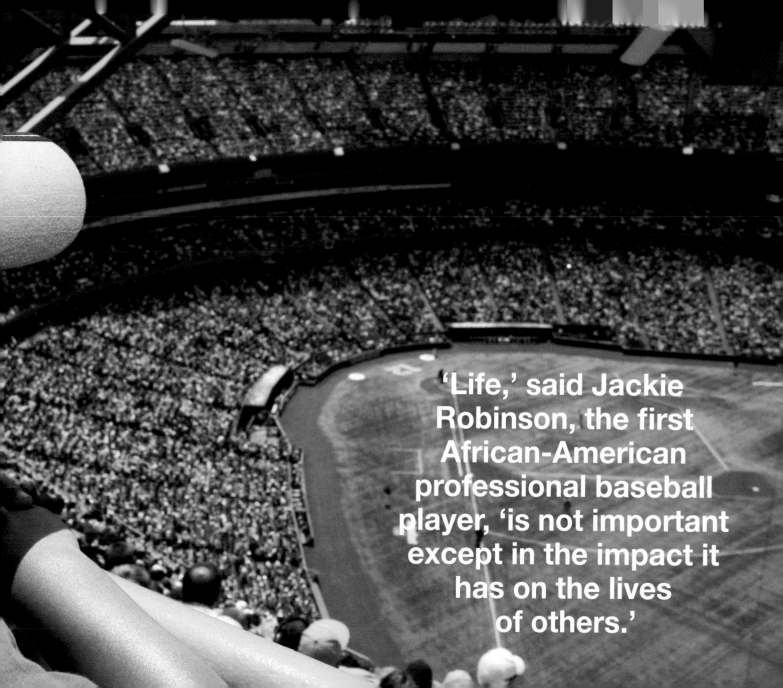

'Life,' said Jackie Robinson, the first African-American professional baseball player, 'is not important except in the impact it has on the lives of others.'

What impact do I want to have on young people? I want them to see that there are 'enablers' and 'disablers'.*

*This comes from the 1989 film *Glory*, based on the story of the 54th Massachusetts Volunteer Infantry – the first formal regiment of African-American soldiers in the US Army during the American Civil War.

There are those who take away your opportunity for growth.

They tell you, you can't.
They tell you, you won't.
They tell you it will never happen.
Or worse, they do it for you.

These are the *disablers*.
They are not evil.
Just misguided.

And then there are *enablers*. People doing it for themselves.

Falling down and getting up.
Learning from that falling.
Changing something.
Learning.
Improving.
Working at it.

And going for it again and again.
And encouraging others to do the same.

Me, I'm an enabler.
'Wow!'
I tell them,
'You're hanging out with the rarest creature on earth, a Black Angel.'

Coach Carter was another Black Angel. You may have seen the film *Coach Carter*. If you haven't, put this book down and go see it. It will help you apply the ideas in this book. He was a Discipline Coach too.

It is a true story set in Los Angeles about a high school basketball team in a black hood. Coach Ken Carter (played by Samuel L. Jackson) is trying to promote change in the face of a culture of low self-esteem and even lower aspirations. His number one tool is getting the team to realize that education is not for school. An education is for life.

The movie shows clearly how family and neighborhood affect behavior in school. It shows students from single parents. It shows students being raised by aunts and uncles or grandparents. It shows how a lack of respect for education is carried from home to school. If you come from a 'bad ass area' then you must be a 'bad ass'.

Coach Carter changes all that.

He addresses them as 'Mr.' – a sign of respect. He sets high academic expectations and sticks to them. He offers extra academic support to help players achieve what they are capable of. He sets up a program where the better students help the weaker ones.

He is applying RAP. He makes changes for a better future.*

In doing so he produces not only academically successful sportsmen but morally sound young men who can go on and make a difference in their families, in their jobs, in their communities.

You see, it's not just about the grades. Young people come to school with their own 'wiring'. (By wiring I mean quite literally the way their brains are wired.) It determines how they think. It determines how they react. And they get this wiring from their home environments.

Coach Carter was a neurosurgeon.

And an electrician.

He rewired children's brains.

How good are you at rewiring children's brains?**

You don't have to do it alone. Maybe.

** Can you rewire your own?

* Yes, it was change they could believe in.

Growing up in New York we had a very close association with the police. They ran weekly sports functions.

They had the Police Athletic League. They taught boxing. They took us to professional games.

Every summer they ran a camp for economically disadvantaged kids. Took them up in the mountains of New York State* for a week of sport and camping out. Great time. I had friends that loved going every year. A safe environment for fun, for meeting new people, for developing social skills. Staffed by the police.

They helped us become good, moral young men and women. Better than just arresting us for our 'behavior'.

* Yes, New York State has mountains!

What can *you* do – today?

THE THEATRE

OF DREAMS

Is your school a **Theatre of Dreams?**

Are you a Miss Potts?

Miss Potts was my fourth grade teacher at Cottle School,
Tuckahoe, New York. Forty-three years ago that was.
Tall lady. Red hair. When I was nine she arranged a visit
to Albany, the state capital. We flew there with Mohawk
Airlines. She was the inspiration for the New York trips I run
for kids from England.

It was on schools trips like this one where I first:

Flew on an airplane

Went up the Empire State Building

Saw the Statue of Liberty

Went to a Broadway play

Visited the Gettysburg Civil War site

Caught a train from Grand Central station

What 'first' have you made happen for your students?

'Firsts' make a difference. New things make new connections.
School rewires children.

New situations.
New challenges.
New opportunities.

Sports. The baking team. The debating team.
The spelling team. The Glee Club.

These all build an ethos of possibility.
School as a Theatre of Dreams.

Schools rewire children.

But they also hardwire children.

Schools remind them they are bad.
Limited.
Stupid.
Hopeless.

And if we don't do anything different, don't let them do
anything different, how will they ever be different?

Things I've been involved in to make a difference:

Creating competitive leagues amongst schools with local press and TV coverage – debating, spelling, cooking, sport.

Connecting with council volunteer programs.

Developing links with local sports teams or local celebrities.

Extra daily help sessions in Math, Science, English, or reading.

Parent education courses to get parents up to date with today's stuff.

Opening your doors to the community and offering creative opportunities that could improve learning for all.

Promoting the school and teachers in a positive light.

Developing a philosophy for the use of your school beyond just teaching children.*

Exposing young people to life and the future – an exciting one, one in which it's their turn to shine.

* It's made of brick. The heat is on. The lights are on.
What can you do to fill it up?

IT TAKES ENERGY

TO COMMIT

Want them to appreciate work?

Then run a Work Appreciation Program.

Where I worked in the south of England the neighborhood had high unemployment and low aspirations for work. So I created the Work Appreciation Program. I wanted to teach students how to work. I wanted to set expectations for work. I wanted to promote work. I wanted them to see how work could develop pride, respect, self-esteem.

So I did a deal with a local bank and got them all accounts. They had a weekly stipend (more than a paper round, less than McDonald's) paid into their own bank account. They could take out up to £20 a day. No more. (Money management is an important life skill.) We had employers like Zurich Insurance Group, IBM, and Portsmouth City Council. We had 250 students working 24 hours a week for four weeks over the summer. We had monitors going round to help ensure students had a proper work experience. Time sheets had to be submitted.

To get in the program all you had to do was attend school for at least 95% of the year. That's inclusive, folks.

Do you have the energy to commit to young people?
Folks, it takes energy to commit.

It takes energy to plan a lesson properly. It takes energy to deal with classroom issues.* It takes energy to come up with new creative ways to learn.

Because if you don't commit to them,

how will they
commit to you?

*It takes even more energy to prevent the issues in the first place.

And if they don't commit to you,

they're not going to
commit to themselves.

And committing
to yourself
is what discipline
is
all
about

We ran the trip to New York in the February half-term. The Work Appreciation Program ran for four weeks in the summer holidays. On the last week of the summer holiday we ran a soccer trip to America. Eight days, playing three games.

Why do I do these things? Because I had teachers and coaches do them for me. These people had 'the art' of making you feel good about yourself.

THE ART –
TO MAKE OTHERS

FEEL GOOD

We all have the power
– **the art** –
to make others feel good.

But how often do we use it?

I have been so blessed to have this art practiced on me by some fantastic teachers and coaches.*

* I like to think of them – and myself – as what I call Humanitarian Foot Soldiers. What about you? If not you, then who?

Mr. Hempel had the art.

He was my high school science teacher. Always smiled. Always said hello in the corridor (no matter how many times he saw you). Always asked after my older sister and cousins. He would come to my house and say good things about how I was getting on in his class at school.

Wow!

Mr. Saunders had the art.

A history teacher. A black guy, one of only two I had in my schooling. He taught me discipline. That how you conduct yourself is vital. He taught me about black people in history – the stuff they didn't teach in other classes. Every year he ran a Year 10 trip to the Gettysburg Civil War site where we had the run of the place.

Wow!

Eli Strand Jr. had the art.

Eli passed away some years ago. He was my mentor. He taught me things. He took me to places. He exposed me to different social situations to help me develop. Eli always talked about what I was capable of. He always talked about my potential.

Wow!

Mr. Hicks had the art.

I played baseball when I was about eight or nine. I was lousy but I remember Mr. Hicks. The more I messed up, the more he told me to stick at it. To try again. When others were criticizing me, he never said a negative thing. I went on to become very good, making three all-star teams including the Daily News first team. Even had a trip to the Yankee Stadium to receive my award. All thanks to Mr. Hicks.

Wow!

Coach R. Griffin had the art.

I attended the University of Rhode Island. I played football for Coach Bob Griffin. He had offered me a scholarship to attend university. Coach Griffin showed class in the way he did things. His dress. His mannerisms. Very educated. He made a myth of the dumb football player. If he had an issue he called you into his office. He spoke to you to let you know what you meant to him and URI football. He talked about education and what a degree would do for you. I was not scheduled to graduate on time. At home I received a call from Coach Griffin: 'Jim, you haven't graduated.' I felt so embarrassed, as though I'd let him down. He invited me back to school. 'We need to finish what we started,' he said. Yo Coach! I owe you. I went back. Graduated. I keep my degree on the wall.

Wow!

Jack Fernandez had the art.

Football coach. Baseball coach. What a man. He was also my PE teacher. He would always acknowledge you wherever he saw you. He would encourage you to play hard. To practice hard. To enjoy the win. I remember him telling me that he liked the pride I took in how I wore my uniform. That, no matter what, my sport shoes were always clean.

Wow!

Coach Priore had the art.

In September 1976 I became the first African-American to attend and play sport at Bronxville High School. I played football, basketball, and baseball earning an all-league mention in three, all-country in two, and Daily News in one. Coach Priore was the first person to tell me that it wasn't a case of whether I would go to university but which one. Playing football for Coach Priore, I had some great days and some not so great. He spoke straight. He didn't treat me like a star on the great days or a failure on the not so great. He helped me get better. He told me what I had to work on. He sent me on recruiting trips to good schools. He wrote recommendations for me, putting his name and coaching reputation on the line. For me.

Wow!

Coach Kuczma had the art.

He was the baseball coach at Bronxville High School. He took us to a number one ranking in Westchester County. First time that had ever happened. He never yelled. He was always smiling. He made conversation with each player. He let me know that I had the choice of football or baseball at the university level. A choice! I remember whenever he was interviewed he always spoke about the players, not himself. Never 'I.' Always 'they' or 'the team.' And, if he mentioned you by name, your parents were so proud.

Wow!

And Miss Potts had the art.

Remember her? Tall lady. Red hair. To raise money for her trips to Albany we worked. Hard. We sold cakes. We washed cars. We raked leaves. What did we learn? Work for what you want. And when you work, work at it. And when you work at it, good things happen. To her, there was no such thing as 'can't afford it.'

Wow!

What did all my teachers and coaches have in common?

Compassion

They identified with my struggle but they always talked about the future. They talked about change. They talked about possibility. They had high expectations.

When it comes to what we
teachers can do, it's endless

but it starts with an ethos.*

*What's yours?

Growing up, I wasn't sure whether going to school would make the difference. Most of us went to school. Our mums made sure of that. It was a question of which school we were lucky enough to find ourselves in. Which ethos we were lucky enough to find ourselves in. (I learned then that ethos is the difference that makes ALL the difference.)

The first high school I went to had an ethos, although I don't think they knew it. It was one of low expectations. Whether kids did well or not didn't really seem to matter. Not their problem. Hey, this is probably as good as it gets. (If you're lucky you might go to college.) They didn't tell us we couldn't. They just never told us we could. The message was, it'll never change. Get over it.

The second school I went to – Bronxville High – had an ethos too. It was that here, all children succeed. Here, we expect great things. From all of you. And from ourselves. It's as good as it gets when you decide it's as good as it gets. (You're lucky because you will go to college - now which one did you have in mind?) Always hope for – and work for – the best. Change is just an obstacle.

Get over it.

Now that's what I call an ethos.

Have you ever seen the TV program *The Garage*?
It made me think.

Shouldn't a school be more like a garage?

When was the last time a garage wrote a car off?

Blamed the car for not starting?

Expected less from it because it came from the wrong side of town?

Saw it as scrap the minute it came in the door?

The Garage ethos?

We sort out any car, no matter what the issue is.*

*In fact, we quite like a challenge. It's what we trained for.

In a school with a Garage ethos it would be:

We sort out any student, no matter the issue.

We equip them with the tools for success in their education.

We equip them with whatever they need to be successful in life.

We create a place students love coming to.

We create a place where they have time and space to get it right.

Where there is no such thing as 'bad' kids.

Where trained 'engineers' give them what they need to change their behavior.

Where, rather than sending children elsewhere, specially trained experts come in and work with the children to address their specific needs.

Where 'engineers' discuss issues and help decide on an action plan for each child.

One that is based on projections!*

*Projections - What do we want the 'end product' to be like? How will we know if we – the teachers and the students – have got it right? Questions like these help to identify projections: What do you want your students to be like when they grow up? What characteristics do you want them to have? How would you define the perfect student? Is this what you are creating now?

Remember, The Garage is a place where they have time and space to get it right.

If a child is rude to a teacher that child gets to spend the day with that teacher.

Or maybe with the caretaker for a day. We don't kick them out.

Sanctions are created to help students learn to change.

Because, remember, The Garage is the place you come to in order to get it right. You are not sent away for not being right when you come through the door.

In The Garage, students are given
opportunities to do the right thing.
If they don't, we teach the right thing.
Then we provide the support and the
space
to get the right thing
right.

And we always,
always

let them know

that we always,
always

expect them to do
the right thing.

We let them know
they can do it.

But what are *they* prepared to do **to do it**?

IT'S A STATE

*When I played baseball I was always number 6, the same as my idol a guy named Ray White who played for the New York Yankees.

OF MIND THING*

After all,

'Life isn't about finding yourself …
… Life is about creating yourself.'

George Bernard Shaw

Discipline coaching is about giving each student
the feeling
that if I put in,
I will
get something out.

That things can change
if I work to change them.
That I can become smarter if I work at it.

That it all starts
with me
starting it.

This willingness to change

To see new possibilities

To be prepared to grow

It's all about their
state of mind.

This is something I've been working on as a coach for 30 years.

Remember those teams that, before anything else, I had to get into a winning state of mind?

I have used this in the classroom as a tool to prepare students for learning.

And as a parent I am constantly working with my children to develop the

'I can'

state of mind.

Then I came across the work of Carol Dweck.*

She is an expert in this state of mind thing.

She calls it 'mindset'.

*See Carol Dweck's *Mindset: The New Psychology of Success* (New York: Ballantine, 2007).

She says that people have either a 'fixed' mindset:
This is the way it is.

It'll never be any different.

Never any better.

This is as good as it gets.
And it ain't that good.*

* I call them the '16-70 crew' - a life spent working. Not achieving.

And then there's the 'growth' mindset people

This is the

Give it a go.
Yes we can.
It might just work.
What's the worst that can happen?
If anyone can, I can.
Let's do it.
Just do it.
Go for it

state of mind.

And, hell, it feels good!

When I work with kids in schools I show them the benefits of having a positive mindset.

A state of mind that means things have the possibility of getting better.

I show them a table like this one:

	Predicted	Actual	Positive
English	B	C	A
Science	A	C	A
Maths	A	D	A
PE	B	C	A
IT	D	D	D

Which clearly shows, folks, you have three choices:

1: Underachieve
Carry on doing what you're doing.

2: Achieve
Work that bit harder and hit the target
your teachers think you are capable of.

3: Overachieve
Do what it takes for as long as it takes.

Your choice

After all,
you choose your state of mind.

Ethos
and
state of mind
fit together

Like a hand in a glove

Your ethos – *yes we can* – is the glove.

Their state of mind – *yes I can* – is the hand.

(Although it works the other way round too.)

My first American football coaching job was at Tuckahoe High School. If you remember, when I started we had won one, lost seven. The following year, we won seven, lost one, drew one. We started a process of change on the very last game of the first season. We decided then that we were going to be good next year. But we had to start working at it now. And that's what we did.

We went out and got t-shirts, new uniforms, new cleets.* We started developing a winning state of mind. We ate dinner together before games. We hung out together. We formed a family around the team. Parents made meals for us. We would go to teammates' homes for dinner and to watch films. We got the state of mind right.

We told them that we can outwork any other team if we practice hard and we're conditioned hard. We started getting busloads of fans following us to games. We created the state of mind that we were worth watching. That we were something special. But we *were* special. The team had schoolwork plus practice and still had to maintain the same grades as non-athletes. That year we went to a bowl game. We had the top quarterback in Westchester. We didn't have a good year. We had a great year.

*Shoes to you.

And, folks, it all started with getting into the right state of mind.

Coach Curras put this poem in my playbook back in 1981.

It's called 'Thinking'.

This is the state of mind that I want for my children.

For my students.

It is the state of mind I want for myself.

If you think you are beaten, you are;
If you think you dare not, you don't.
If you'd like to win, but think you can't
It's almost a cinch you won't.
If you think you'll lose, you've lost,
For out in the world we find
Success being with a fellow's will;
It's all in the state of mind.

If you think you're outclassed, you are:
You've got to think high to rise.
You've got to be sure of yourself before
You can ever win a prize.
Life's battles don't always go
To the stronger or faster man,
But soon or late the man who wins
Is the one who thinks he can.

Walter D. Wintle

DRIVING CHANGE

Talking of states of mind …

Are you an **eagle**

or

an **oyster**?

Are you a **driver**

or

a **rider**?

Your answer can

change

everything.

An eagle must take care of its young. It must feed itself and them. It must keep itself clean and in good shape for hunting. It must make sure it inhabits a good hunting ground.

It must fight for the best hunting ground.

Home, if you are an eagle, is where some of the worst weather is found.

It takes a lot of effort to be a good eagle.

An oyster, on the other hand just sits in the same spot all its life.

With its mouth open eating grit.*

*Chances of an oyster coming up with a pearl? About one in a million. You've got to sit and swallow a lot of grit to 'strike it lucky'!

And are you a driver or a rider?

Drivers are people who work
at change.
They take responsibility.
They don't just sit and watch.

If they're not happy with the
way things are,
they do something about it.

They are in control of where
they are going
and how they are going
to get there.

Riders,
on the other hand,
go where drivers take them.

And moan.

I read a lot. My specialty is African history and its relationship to African-American culture. I discovered my history started long before slavery. Through my research I've learned about some people who had the will to make change happen. These folks didn't just talk about change. They promoted change. They were the drivers. I like to think I'm descended from drivers. My mentor, Eli Strand, once told me that because one of my ancestors survived a slave ship, that makes me one of the strongest of my kind. Wow! See, folks, you need strength to drive. You need a state of mind that promotes the idea that you too can be a driver.

Booker T. Washington (1856–1915) was a driver. He was born at a time when educating black people was not a priority in the United States. But he had other plans. Booker T. felt that an education was the single most important tool for change for African-Americans. If we were ever to be respected we had 'to be educated'. He had to work while studying at Hampton Institute for freedmen. At this time, African-American students went to all-African-American schools, and there were very few such schools. In 1881 Booker T. was selected to be the Head of the Tuskegee Institute. He built Tuskegee into a great college for higher learning. He was very much a driver. No excuses. This is what needs to be done. And I'm going to do something!

'We can't all do everything, but everyone can do something.'

George Bernard Shaw*

*Another driver. He once said, 'A life spent making mistakes is not only more honourable but more useful than a life spent doing nothing'.

EXPLOITING

OPPORTUNITY

Eagles and drivers have something else in common

They know an opportunity
when they see it

And when they see it
they take it

Despite being born in the United States in the 1950s during a climate of serious racial discrimination and prejudice, my life has been a succession of opportunities with one thing in common – education.

Miss Potts gave me the opportunity to fly in an airplane that helped me develop a passion for learning.

That gave me the opportunity

To be the first African-American to attend and play sport at Bronxville High School.

Black Tuckahoe gridder will play at Bronxville

JIM ROBERSON
. . . Bronxville

Bronxville came out smoking in the second half, re-covering its onside kick and moving the ball to the Croton 28 behind the running of Jimmy Roberson and Jack Con-nors. The Bronco bid died, however, when tackle Larry Flannery was tagged with an illegal man downfield penal-ty and Bronxville was later penalized for offensive pass interference.

Agony of defeat

Roger Goodell of Bronxville makes a tackle on Croton's Dough Garbarini (top) and Jim Ro-berson of Bronxville (bottom) looks for daylight

Bronxville's Jim Roberson on his way to the basket

Up and over

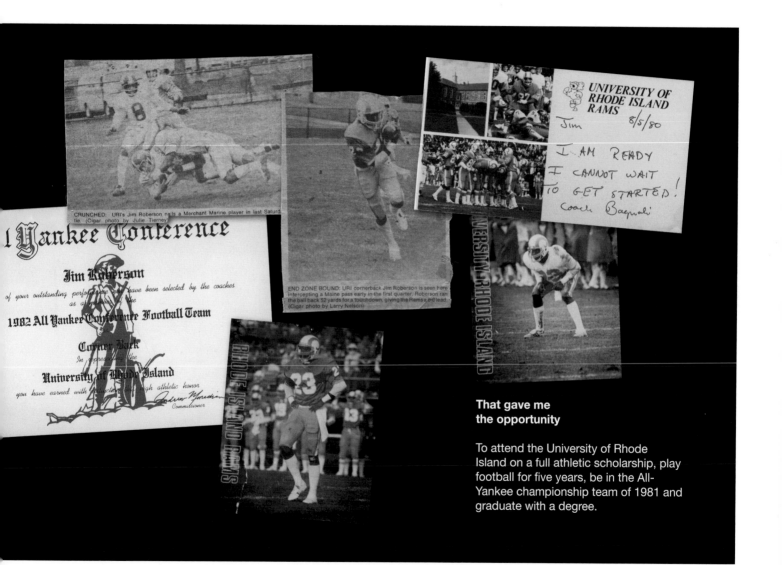

CRUNCHED: URI's Jim Roberson nails a Merchant Marine player in last Saturd... tie. (Cigar photo by Julie Tierney)

END ZONE BOUND: URI cornerback Jim Roberson is seen here intercepting a Maine pass early in the first quarter. Roberson ran the ball back 52 yards for a touchdown, giving the Rams a 6-0 lead. (Cigar photo by Larry Nelson)

UNIVERSITY OF RHODE ISLAND RAMS 8/5/80

Jim

I AM READY I CANNOT WAIT TO GET STARTED!

Coach Baepuali

Yankee Conference

Jim Roberson

of your outstanding performance have been selected by the coaches as a member of the

1982 All Yankee Conference Football Team

Corner Back

In representing the

University of Rhode Island

you have earned with distinction high athletic honor

Commissioner

That gave me the opportunity

To attend the University of Rhode Island on a full athletic scholarship, play football for five years, be in the All-Yankee championship team of 1981 and graduate with a degree.

That gave me
the opportunity

To coach high school football in New York state.

That gave me
the opportunity

To become a Head Coach in my first-ever coaching job.

That gave me
the opportunity

To learn firsthand how you go from a record of 1–7 to 7–1, the opportunity to develop young men into champions, and the opportunity to win a bowl game.

All of which
**gave me
the opportunity**

To return to the University of Rhode Island
as an Assistant Coach and Junior Varsity
Coach.

**That gave me
the opportunity**

To come to England to coach American
football (where I met my lovely wife) and,
because I had a university degree, I had
the opportunity to teach at a school in
England and to develop the Discipline
Coach ideas.

And this experience of working with
young people across the UK gave me the
opportunity for my wife and me to start
up our own company, Youth Minded,* to
work with Ian Gilbert and those nice folks
at Independent Thinking, and to showcase
my work in the book you have in your
hand.

* Motto: 'Creating aspirations for life'.

Thanks, Miss Potts – if you only knew what you'd started!

Every opportunity
is an
opportunity

to develop
to change
to grow
to improve
to start afresh.

To start. Period.

And some opportunities
change everything.

Like the black soldier in the Second World War who wanted the opportunity to fight and not just bake bread. Or Malcolm X talking about the opportunity African-Americans should have to go to good schools, to have good homes, to have access to good hospitals. The same opportunities as white folks.

My father told me I had the opportunity to break down myths about African-Americans. Since I was the first African-American friend some Bronxville kids had, an opportunity to let them see how we lived, how we ate, to taste the food my mum made, to show them we are human beings just like them, trying to make it just like them.*

So I know from first hand that equal opportunities create other opportunities.

News photo by Leonard Detrick
Jim Roberson, Roger Goodell and Al Schnoor cause pitchers lots of problems.

*Roger Goodell, the NFL Commissioner, was one of those kids who came to my house to eat with us

And education is the biggest opportunity of them all.

What are you doing as a teacher
to encourage young people
to take opportunities?

What are you doing as a teacher
to give them opportunities?

What can you do now, having read
this book, to help them develop the
discipline to see opportunities, to take
opportunities, and to follow through on
those opportunities?

To develop the discipline
to be all they can be?

To be their own **Discipline Coach**?

I'm less like a friend and
more like a parent.

And I'm less like a president and
more like a general.

And I'm less like a rider and
more like a driver.

And I'm less like a problem and
more like a solution.

And I'm less like a mechanic and
more like an engineer.

And I'm less like an oyster and
more like an eagle.

And I'm less like a caretaker and
more like an architect.

I am **The Discipline Coach.**

Image Credits

All images are from the author's personal scrapbook with the exception of the following:

www.**TheDisciplineCoach**.co.uk